ADVANCED DRILLS & GOALIE DRILLS
— FOR —
HOCKEY

Dr. Randy Gregg

OVER
TIME
BOOKS

The Publisher: OverTime Books is an imprint of Éditions de la Montagne Verte

Library and Archives Canada Cataloguing in Publication

Gregg, Randy, 1956–
    Advanced drills & goalie drills for hockey / Randy Gregg.

    ISBN-13: 978-09737681-8-3
    ISBN-10: 0-9737681-8-5

    1. Hockey—Coaching. I. Title.

GV848.3.G745 2006   796.962077   C2006-904206-3

Project Director: J. Alexander Poulton
Illustrator: Ross Palsson
Cover Image: Dave Vasicek, ColorSpace Photo-Graphics

PC:P5

Contents

Dedication: To my daughter Sarah, whose combination of incredible mental focus and respect for teammates and opposition players alike reminds me that sport can be played at an elite level in an atmosphere of respect and focused competition and that mental focus is key to success of an athlete and a team

Skills-Based Learning

LIKE MOST TEAM SPORTS, HOCKEY IS AN INTEGRATED GAME.
Players must learn the individual skills necessary to be
a competent player. A young athlete must then learn how to
use these skills in a team environment so that team performance is maximized. As a player progresses to a more competitive hockey environment, there is an increased emphasis
on physical conditioning using on-ice and dryland training.
However, in addition to skill mastery and the physical part of
the game, it is mental strength that can often separate elite
hockey players from true superstars.

Although the individual abilities of hockey players vary
widely from youth to adolescence to adulthood, the skills
they must possess to become better are similar. There
are 10 skills that are of primary importance in the development of a hockey player. These include skating speed,
agility, power, stickhandling, passing, shooting, checking,
positional play, intuition and
work ethic. It is important
to emphasize the devel-
opment of these skills at
every practice.

In organized minor hockey,
players are seldom
coached by the
same person for
more than one
season. Inevitably,
each year players
must adapt to yet
another coaching

style and temperament. This may not be such a bad thing because it gives the young players a wide range of experience so they can judge for themselves what type of coach or practice makes them perform at optimal levels. However, the main problem with exposing young players to a different coach every year is the variability in how each one teaches the 10 fundamental hockey skills.

An analogy with formal schooling is appropriate. Does a Grade Four math teacher develop and teach a system of learning to calculate fractions only to have the Grade Five teacher create a completely new system? Of course not. The school system was developed with an organized, consistent approach to learning so that students get the best chance to excel in all the subjects. Curricula are established and then closely followed by teachers from year to year so that every child has an equal opportunity to learn.

In hockey, well-meaning and enthusiastic volunteers give their time freely "to help the kids." Without volunteer coaching ranks, it would not be possible for the vast majority of youngsters to play hockey. Thirty years ago, Father David Bauer believed that it would be best if hockey was integrated into the school system to ensure consistent instruction for all players. Over the years there have been a number of excellent programs for coaches to become even better teachers on the ice. I hope that this manual can provide some valuable tools that will make this directed focus on teaching at practice even more successful.

SKILLS-BASED
LEARNING

How to Use this Book

IN VIRTUALLY EVERY ASPECT OF SOCIETY, PREPARATION and planning are two vital steps toward success in any endeavor. Teachers prepare lesson plans for their daily classes, doctors prepare for surgical procedures and truck drivers plan their routes before embarking on a trip. Similarly, it is imperative that coaches plan and prepare for each practice. Having an overall objective for each practice is essential. The objective for a particular practice may be skating, breakouts, power play or defensive zone play, but it is important that the objectives for individual practices also further the overall goal of building a team that works well together. It is important to select practice drills that best suit the needs of the team at that particular stage of the season. This book describes many integrated drills that can be used to develop a strong practice plan. Skating, puck control and team drills can be found in Books 1–3.

Five Guidelines for Practice Planning

When developing a practice plan, follow these five main guidelines in order to maximize a team's practice potential:

1.	Be prepared—make a practice plan.
2.	Use progressive skill learning through drill expansion.
3.	Work on each individual skill during each practice.
4.	Use technical and dynamic drills in appropriate situations.
5.	Make practices fun.

Be prepared—make a practice plan

Coaches expect every player to come to practice with skates, stick and other equipment in hand, ready to work hard for the entire one-hour practice. Similarly, players and parents should expect the coaching staff to be ready to run an effective, well-organized practice with drills that challenge and stimulate players in every position. As in many other teaching professions, a written plan is a valuable tool for two reasons:

1. Making a practice plan requires that a coach spend time the night before thinking about the strengths and weaknesses of his team and how it can improve. Then the coach can choose specific drills to focus on learning in those areas of weakness. A written practice plan is easy to follow and provides a focus for the practice, ensuring that ice time is used most efficiently.

2. Watching a coach who regularly checks his written plan gives parents in the stands confidence that the practice has been well thought through and will be worthwhile for their children. Demonstrating a high level of preparation is an important step to gaining parents' confidence towards the decisions made during each game of the season.

Use progressive skill learning through drill expansion

Shortly after retiring from the National Hockey League, I had the opportunity to coach my young sons in organized youth hockey. Although it was quite obvious that their skill level was low, I tried the same drills that I had used in NHL practices. Of course, I had to scale back both the complexity and intensity of the drills to fit the level of my little team. I was pleased to see that, not only did these young seven- and eight-year-olds pick up the idea behind the drills quickly, but practices were high paced, fun and a wealth of learning for the players. I realized then that the skills of hockey are no different whether at the atom or the professional level. It was simply a matter of establishing the level of complexity that could be handled by the players in question. The concept of drill expansion was born. It excited me to think that young hockey players could go through their entire minor hockey experience practicing a set of drills that were consistent yet constantly expanding in intensity and complexity. Novice players, Bantam players and Olympians can use a similar set of drills that provide a consistent approach to teaching the skills of the game. This idea is, of course, no different than what the school system did years ago when they developed standardized teaching curricula in the core school subjects so that all students benefit from formal education. That has always sounded like a worthy goal for hockey organizations. However, because the system relies on volunteer coaches who have diverse backgrounds and who often change from year to year, the idea of a common coaching strategy with regards to practice organization is still in its infancy.

The Canadian Hockey Association and USA Hockey have done a remarkable job in developing coaching seminars and clinics to provide coaches with a stronger background in hockey knowledge. This book is intended to be a useful, practical tool for coaches interested in offering the best practices available to their players. Sample practice plans and practice templates have been included in the book to make it easy for a coach at any hockey level to expand his skills in practice planning and organization. Refer to *Skating Drills for Hockey* (Book 1), *Puck Control Drills for Hockey* (Book 2) and *Team Drills for Hockey* (Book 3) for other drills to complete your practice.

Work on each individual skill during each practice

Having a major theme or objective in mind is a good idea when planning a hockey practice. If the team is struggling with passing or defensive positioning, then it would be productive to include specific drills that focus on those areas. It is also important to consider including at least one drill to work each of the specific individual hockey skills while progressing through practice. Following a good warmup, it is important to work on skating, stickhandling, passing, shooting and checking skills in every practice before requiring players to perform the more dynamic team-oriented drills. It has been said a solid house is built on a strong foundation, and there is no doubt that the foundation of a good hockey player is the mastery of individual technical skills!

Use technical and dynamic drills effectively

Because teaching the various aspects of the game of hockey can be complicated in both its individual and team responsibilities, it is important that coaches help players develop new skills in a slow and progressive way. Attempting to teach a sophisticated defensive breakout system to a group of first-year players is a recipe for disaster. Fortunately, most hockey skills can be taught in two ways—technically and dynamically.

In this manual you will notice that the drills are divided into two basic groupings:

- **Technical drills** are designed to decrease the complexity of the rink environment so that players can focus totally on one specific skill. This is a time when coaches can easily approach individual players to work on teaching changes to their technique in a particular area. A good example of a technical drill would be the Stationary Pass Drill, where players stand in one location working with a partner on receiving and making good passes.

- **Dynamic drills** are designed to integrate the exciting aspects of hockey, including speed, finesse, positional play and checking. These drills are effective in developing the same individual technical skills but are set in an environment that more closely resembles a regular game setting. Because these drills are run at a faster pace, several external stimuli are present that challenge each player to be even more aware of the entire game setting. Do not try dynamic drills until all players have almost mastered the technical drills that teach similar hockey skills in isolation. For more experienced players, this kind of drill most closely simulates game situations where many things are happening on the ice at one time.

Drill Favorites Icon: Several drills in the book are identified with this icon. These are my favorite drills in each of the skill sections. They are drills that are applicable at any age level in hockey, and I strongly recommend them to any coach. Even the best hockey coach does not need thousands of drills in order to improve his team. He simply needs a core of 10 or 20 drills that he feels comfortable with to properly develop his players' individual and team skills.

Level of Difficulty Icon: All of the drills in this book have been assigned a level of difficulty, which provides a sense of how and when a particular drill should be included in planning a practice. A drill with Level 1 difficulty can be easily carried out by beginning players, while a drill with Level 4 difficulty is quite complex and should be reserved for more experienced, competitive players.

It is necessary to first evaluate the level of talent on the team. From that assessment, determine the level of difficulty that is most appropriate for the drills to include in a practice plan.

Make practices fun

There continues to be a small group of coaches, managers and parents who believe that players cannot develop the ultimate commitment to hockey if they have fun during practice. A smiling, joking player who enjoys the social aspect of hockey to the same degree as he enjoys the physical aspect has in the past been looked upon as being soft or lacking discipline. Luckily, this attitude is quickly going the way of the dinosaur!

For the vast majority of amateur hockey players, the number one reason why they play hockey is to have fun with their friends. Although many dream of a professional career, the reality for most is that success will likely be measured by simply continuing through the minor hockey ranks and enjoying the game so much that they continue to play into adulthood. Hockey is a fine game with its speed, finesse, tactics and emphasis on teamwork. Every child who is interested should have the opportunity to participate in the game at a level that is best suited for him skillwise, socially, and financially.

Coaches who berate players, punish them with excessive skating or who verbally criticize young referees in front of their teams have little grasp of the great influence they really have on their players. Hockey continues to struggle to keep its players from turning to sports that offer recreation at a lower cost. Many hockey experts believe that a major turnaround in attitude towards the teaching of hockey is needed in order to return hockey to its position of glory in the cultural makeup of our country.

So what can a coach do to ensure that each player on his team enjoys the sport of hockey to its utmost? From a psychological standpoint, there are many ways a coach can help build self-esteem, create a non-threatening dressing room environment, and assist in developing long-term friendships among the team members. Unfortunately, this topic is outside the scope of this book. For further details and a more comprehensive reference on coaching philosophy, injury identification, proper nutrition and skill enhancement, please refer to *Hockey: The Technical, the Physical, and the Mental Game.**

Every morning on a game day, National Hockey League teams have a pre-game skate. It is usually just a quick workout so that players can stretch out and work on some flow drills before the evening game. During my time with the Edmonton Oilers, the real practice often began once the coaches left the ice. Players would surround the center ice circle and begin a rousing game of Pig in the Middle. We would play that game for what seemed like hours, working on our passing and receiving, but mostly just having a great time. The memories of players like Gretzky and Messier laughing and joking during the simple game that I now use with my young teams will stay with me forever. Many people wonder why some players become truly great superstars. Part of the puzzle is undoubtedly physical talent, but I am sure that a big part of hockey success also comes from this intense love of playing the game.

---

* *Hockey: The Technical, the Physical, and the Mental Game* by Dr. Randy Gregg. ©1999, FP Hendriks Publishing Ltd.

During practices coaches can do several things to ensure that players enjoy their hockey experience:

1. **Have a positive attitude.**
   Every hockey player makes mistakes. If we focus on what people can do rather than what they can't, then we develop willing and eager players.

2. **Maintain a high tempo at practice.**
   One easy way that players lose interest in the game is when they must endure a poorly organized and boring practice. Make it fast and make it fun!

3. **Lead by example; be energetic.**
   It's hard for a player to give all he has if his coach and role model is lethargic, bored and appears to be disinterested.

4. **Be fair.**
   The quickest way to lose your players' respect is to show favoritism to your own child or to the players on the team who are more skilled.

5. **Run practices efficiently.**
   The main reason coaches must extend practices for minor hockey players past one hour is because they are not well prepared. Short, high-tempo practices make for good skill challenges and happy players!

6. **Include at least one fun drill at the end of practice.**
   Would you rather have your players spend the three or four days before next practice remembering how sick they felt after a hard punishing skate, or would you rather they remember the excitement and fun of playing a challenging game that also helped to improve their hockey skills? The answer seems obvious to most. Please refer to Chapter 4 for some effective ideas that can be used during each practice.

A Note about Male and Female Hockey

You will notice throughout this book that I use the words *he*, *him*, and *his* when describing hockey players and coaches. I do this only for ease of reading, not because of a bias towards male dominance in hockey. It is exciting to see the number of female hockey teams sprouting up in amateur hockey leagues across the country, as well as the development of many very capable and experienced female coaches. Hockey is the type of dynamic, fast-paced game that should be enjoyed by all youngsters, big or small, rich or poor, skilled or inexperienced, male or female. It is encouraging to see interest in female hockey increase, from novice levels all the way up to participation in the Olympic Games!

Even the best hockey coach does not need thousands of drills in order to improve his team. He simply needs a core of 10 or 20 drills that he feels comfortable with to properly develop his players' individual and team skills.

Integrated Play

A YOUNG PLAYER MUST ATTAIN MANY MILESTONES IN ORDER to become a competent hockey player. The first milestone is to master the skill of skating. Players then proceed to gain confidence in puckhandling, passing, shooting and checking. Overall, a hockey player with all these skills can quite easily compete at the top levels of his age group. However, to become an elite player, young athletes must learn to use these physical skills and combine them with positional play, intuition and work ethic in order to become a complete hockey player.

This is one of the most exciting aspects of the game. It is not the biggest nor the fastest nor the best passing team that wins the game. Championship teams are formed by the universal resolve that every player understands and works on an integrated approach to becoming the best players they can be.

The elements of an integrated approach to playing hockey are:

- · power plays,
- · penalty killing, and
- · transitional skills.

This book also contains a section of drills for goalies as well as game drills in which players can practice all the skills they have learned in an integrated environment.

Power Play/Penalty Killing

Definition—*the ability to use odd-man situations during a game to your team's advantage*

AS GAMES BECOME MORE COMPETITIVE AND CHALLENGING FOR the players, it is often the small components that can make the difference between winning and losing. There is no question that teams that excel during man-advantage situations have a distinct edge over their opposition.

Young hockey players must spend a considerable amount of time improving the individual skills of skating, stickhandling, passing and shooting. When it comes to odd-man situations, young players may have a hard time grasping more complex team strategies. Experienced coaches often teach one simple power play and penalty-killing strategy that their players can practice regularly and use in games. As the players get older, coaches can increase the complexity of these strategies.

Power play and penalty-killing drills are specialty drills that are not designed to be used regularly during practice. They should be considered in the event that a team would benefit from refreshing their ideas on proper positioning, breakouts and team strategy. Coaches often identify parts of a hockey season where man-advantage situations are not working well for their team. By incorporating a step-by-step review of power play and penalty-killing principles into a team practice, experienced coaches can often reverse their team's fortunes in these important game situations.

On the following pages are drills that focus on power play and penalty-killing skills.

POWER PLAY/
PENALTY KILLING

Power Play Offensive Breakouts

Objective
To practice full-ice breakouts under proper control

Description
- Line up one set of five players at center ice as if there is a face-off.
- Start the play by dumping a puck into the defensive corner.
- A defenseman controls the puck behind the net while the center swings into one corner.
- The defenseman makes a lateral pass to the center, then one or two more passes are made between the forwards before the offensive blue line.
- Once inside the offensive blue line, the forwards set up in the offensive zone, passing between each other and finishing the play with a shot on goal.

Key Teaching Points
- Encourage full team integration with good timing.
- Emphasize several defensive and mid-ice zone options.
- Promote good communication between teammates.

EXPANSION

Add one forechecker, then two forecheckers to apply pressure during the breakout.

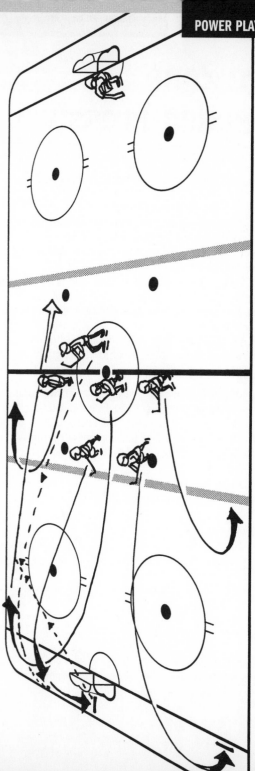

Offensive Zone Short-Handed Pressure

Objective

To develop proper swing movement for short-handed forecheckers

Description

- Line up a five-man offensive unit and two forecheckers at center ice.
- Start the play by dumping a puck into the defensive corner.
- The defenseman gets control of the puck and sets up behind the net, with the center swinging into one corner.
- The first forechecker swings with the center, then angles back to the middle of the rink.
- The second forechecker pressures the puck carrier or follows the movement of the first pass.
- Both players enter the defensive zone in the middle of the rink.
- Play continues with a shot on goal after which the next group begins.

Key Teaching Points

- Encourage integration of two-man coverage in the offensive zone.
- Emphasize that it is important not to get caught deep with the first offensive pass.
- Forwards should practice both offensive and forechecking roles.

EXPANSION

Add two defensemen for a stronger defensive challenge.

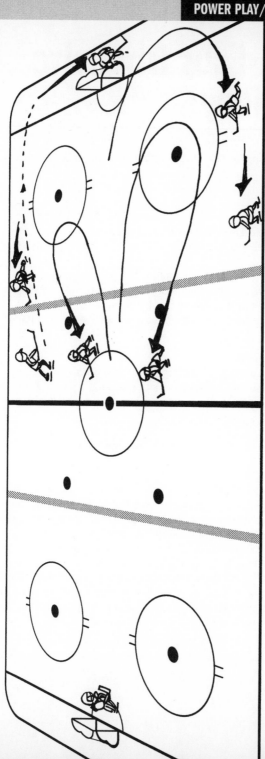

**OFFENSIVE ZONE
SHORT-HANDED PRESSURE**

Five-on-Four Offensive Power Play

Objective
To develop quick, effective offensive zone passing with mild defensive resistance

Description
- Set up a five-on-four play in the offensive zone.
- Four defensive players hold their sticks by the blade so that there is less potential passing interference and to make power-play passing easier.
- Start the drill by dumping a puck into a defensive corner.
- The offensive players gain control of the puck and make plays to penetrate the box by quickly passing the puck.
- Progress with a variety of plays. These are described on the following pages.

Key Teaching Points
- Encourage good anticipation before receiving a pass.
- Promote intelligent box penetration with passes.

EXPANSION

Defensive players use their sticks properly with the blade on the ice.

#1. High Triangle
- Set up a triangle of offensive players in the offensive zone, usually with a defenseman just inside the blue line in the middle of the ice, his partner on one side of the ice at the top of the corner circle and a forward located at the top of the other circle.
- Have the deep forwards switch from being in the offensive corners when passing to quickly skating to the front of the net and taking a point shot. The top three players pass among each other forming the high triangle. When they catch a defensive player out of position, they can skate quickly through a seam that has formed in the defense and take a shot from a dangerous position.

FIVE-ON-FOUR OFFENSIVE POWER PLAY

#2. Side Triangle

- Set up a triangle of offensive players in the offensive zone. Usually the center controls the puck, standing near the boards at the hash marks of one of the offensive circles. A defenseman positions himself just inside the blue line closer to the middle of the ice, and a forward is deep in the same-side offensive corner.
- The opposing forward usually sets up in front of the net and the opposing defenseman lines up inside the blue line directly in the middle of the ice.
- The three side players pass among themselves, in the side triangle, until a defensive player is caught out of position. An offensive player then quickly skates through the seam that has formed in the defense and takes a shot from a dangerous position.

#3. Behind-the-Net Play

- Sometimes in the Side Triangle setup, the penalty killers are very disciplined, and it is impossible to get the defenders to commit out of their penalty-killing positions.
- In order to force the defensive players to give up their stable positions, the deep corner forward passes behind the net to the opposite forward, who leaves his position in front of the net and retrieves the pass.
- The entire power-play unit shifts position to the opposite side of the rink where they then set up the Side Triangle play again and hope the penalty-killing unit is more vulnerable.
- In most cases, the key player in the Side Triangle formation is the center who controls the puck at the side. It is an advantage to have him on the side of the ice where he can make a direct forehand shot on goal if required. That is, a left-shooting center should try to set up on the right side of the offensive zone, and a right-shooting center should try to set up on the left side.

FIVE-ON-FOUR
OFFENSIVE POWER PLAY

#4. Back Side Passing Play

The Back Side Passing Play is an effective option that teams can use from a Side Triangle formation.

- If the penalty-killing unit tends to overplay the strong side of the ice where the puck is located, the Back Side Passing Play begins by having the opposite defenseman skate hard through the slot area.
- He must time his arrival so that he reaches the slot when the deep winger or center has control of the puck and is prepared to pass.
- If no defensive player goes to cover the defenseman, the center or deep winger passes to the defenseman, who makes a quick shot on goal from the slot.
- If, however, the defensive team responds by having their far defenseman come to cover the defenseman skating through the slot, then the opposite offensive forward can pivot to the high slot area and receive a crisp pass for a dangerous shot on goal, in effect, creating a second back side passing option.

This play creates a two-on-one offensive play against the defenseman covering the dangerous slot area. Even if this play is not successful, it is often effective in opening up the defensive box as players begin to be more aware of these dangerous back side plays.

EXPANSION

Defensive players use their sticks properly with the blade on the ice.

**FIVE-ON-FOUR
OFFENSIVE POWER PLAY**

Four-Man Box Rotation

Objective
To become consistent with a tightly controlled penalty-killing box formation

Description
- Line four players up in a defensive box formation in the end zone.
- Point to a corner of the ice or a blue-line area as if an imaginary puck has been shot there. Players react to the movement of the puck by skating to the proper defensive position.
- Practice five or six transitions to various positions in the defensive zone, then switch players and repeat the drill.
- Stop the defensive rotations to show proper player positioning as necessary.
- Extra players practice individual drills, face-offs or shot blocking in the mid-ice zone until it is their turn.

Key Teaching Points
- Emphasize that it is important to react to other teammates' positions.
- Emphasize that players must always try to stay in good defensive positions and not get caught out of the box formation.
- Promote a great deal of communication between defensive teammates.

**FOUR-MAN
BOX ROTATION**

Three-Man Triangle Rotation

Objective
To develop an effective rotational system when penalty killing five-on-three

Description
- Line three players up in a defensive triangle in the end zone.
- Point to one defensive corner or to the blue-line area on the ice as if an imaginary puck has been shot there. Players react to the change in puck location by repositioning themselves in an effective defensive position.
- The three-man penalty-killing system is usually set up as follows: the front two players, usually forwards, move up and back on either side of the slot area. The back defenseman always stays in front of the net but favors the side of the net where the puck is located.
- Practice five or six transitions to various puck positions on the ice, then switch players and repeat the drill.
- Stop the defensive rotations at any time and instruct the players as to the proper positions as necessary.
- Extra players practice individual skills, face-offs or long passing in the mid-ice zone until it is their turn.

Key Teaching Points
- Encourage tight positioning in the defensive zone.
- Encourage players to react to puck movement for proper ice position in the zone.

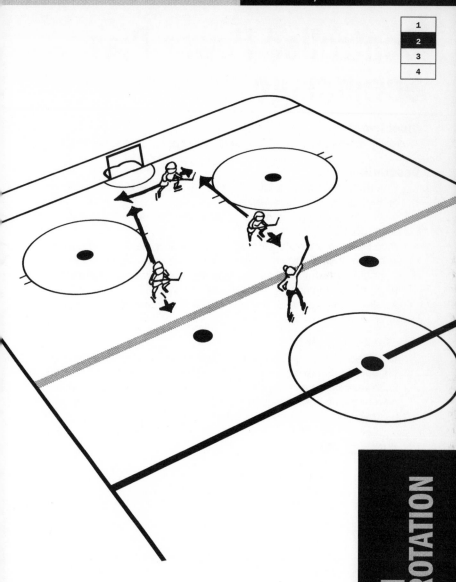

1
2
3
4

**THREE-MAN
TRIANGLE ROTATION**

Controlled Power Play Scrimmage

Objective
To provide teaching opportunities during active power play scrimmages

Description
- Line two teams up for a face-off at center ice—one with five skaters and the other with four skaters.
- Begin the scrimmage by dropping the puck or dumping it into the defensive zone.
- Stop play at any time by blowing the whistle; players stop immediately when they hear the whistle and maintain their positions on the ice.
- Point out problems or possible strategies for improved performance.
- Begin the scrimmage again by blowing the whistle.
- As play progresses, stop the flow of play less frequently and allow more spontaneous play.

Key Teaching Points
- Encourage the team that is on the power play to keep two players on the puck at all times.
- Encourage the team that is killing the penalty to try to keep offensive players on the outer edges of the rink with no access to the dangerous mid-slot area in front of the net.

EXPANSION

Play five-on-three power play situations.

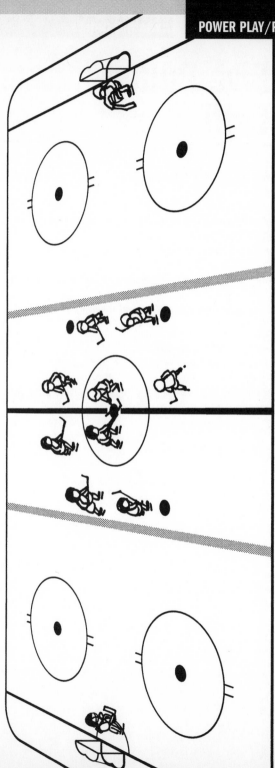

CONTROLLED POWER PLAY SCRIMMAGE

Six-on-Five Pulled Goalie Drill

Objective
To develop coordinated last-minute offensive plays

Description
- Line up teams of six against five at center ice for a face-off.
- Start the play with a pass to an offensive player.
- Encourage the attacking team to always have two players close to the puck.
- The offensive team tries to jam the front of the net when they take a shot.
- Switch players from defense to offense every few minutes.

Key Teaching Points
- Encourage puck control with good passes.
- Encourage aggressive checking to regain puck control.
- It is vital with a six-on-five pulled goalie attack that two offensive players always commit to the puck area, effectively outmanning the opposition all over the ice.

SIX-ON-FIVE PULLED GOALIE DRILL

Transition Skills

Definition—*the ability to quickly change from a defensive to an offensive team strategy*

AS THE GAME OF HOCKEY CONTINUES TO EVOLVE AS a fast-paced, dynamic sport, rapid counterattacks in the mid-ice zone have become effective ways to develop scoring opportunities. Teams can acquire specific team-oriented skills that allow them to take advantage of times in a game where puck possession changes quickly.

During my playing days with the Edmonton Oilers in the 1980s, the game of hockey changed dramatically. Prior to the domination of the game by players such as Gretzky, Jagr, Bure and others, the physical nature of the game was very important. Traveling into Philadelphia to play the Flyers meant we were in for a battle all over the ice, whether in front of the net or in the defensive and offensive corners. Games were won on toughness, good positional play and turning offensive opportunities into goals.

In the 1990s teams began to realize that a high-speed game that focused on finesse, pinpoint passing and a strong transition game in the neutral zone could be just as effective as the more physical strategy. Plus, it was a lot more fun to play! The Russians and other European teams had shown us for years how important transitional skills were to become a great team, and this focus has now become vital to the success of every National Hockey League team.

On the following pages are drills that focus on transition skills.

TRANSITION SKILLS

Pairs Passing Transition

Objective

To develop quick transitions from backward skating to forward skating while maintaining puck control

Description

- Pair up players and line the pairs up across the rink, approximately 3 meters (9 feet) apart.
- Each pair has a puck, and the puck handler begins by skating forward.
- His partner skates backward, receives a pass, stops and begins to skate forward.
- The first player stops after making the first pass and begins skating backward to receive the return pass.
- Start and stop the drill with a whistle so that you can ensure that the players work at full intensity for only 15 to 20 seconds.

Key Teaching Points

- Promote quick feet and heads always up.
- Encourage fast transitions from one direction to the other.
- Encourage good passes directly onto the receiver's stick.
- Players should concentrate on stopping using both skate edges and maintaining good puck control using the stick.

EXPANSION

Players try saucer passes and backhand passes during the drill.

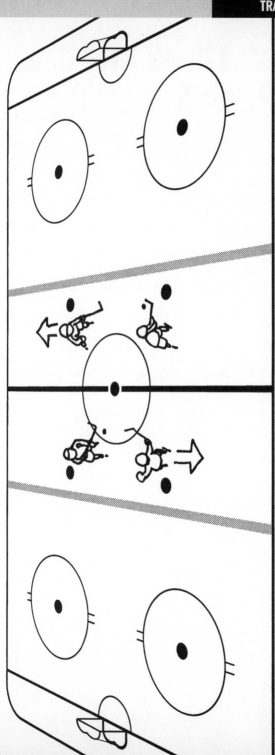

PAIRS PASSING TRANSITION

Three-on-Three Mid-Ice Three-Puck Scrimmage

Objective

To encourage quick transitions from defense to offense and vice versa

Description

- Position the two nets back to back at center ice with two teams lined up along respective blue lines.
- The first three players on each team line up in front of their own goaltender.
- The extra players spread out across the blue lines and get ready for passes from the active players.
- Start the game by dropping three pucks in various areas of the ice between the blue lines.
- Players try to score on the opposing goaltender. They can use their blue line teammates for give-and-go passes.
- The first team to score two goals wins.
- Once a team scores two goals, three new players from the blue line skate into the middle to become the active players and repeat the drill.

Key Teaching Points

- Encourage aggressive puck pursuit and full awareness of puck position.
- Encourage quick changes from defense to offense and good anticipation.

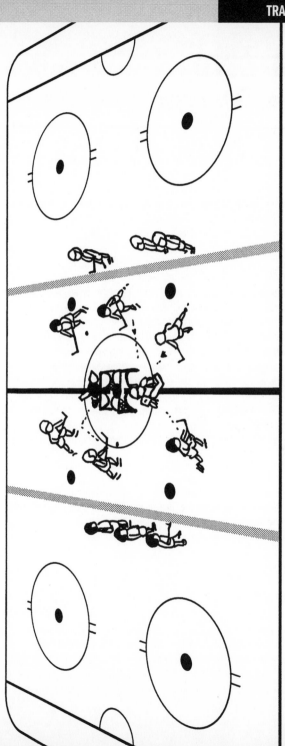

THREE-ON-THREE MID-ICE THREE-PUCK SCRIMMAGE

Five-on-Zero Mid-Ice Regroup

Objective
To develop effective five-man regrouping skills in the neutral zone

Description
- Defensemen and forwards line up in an offensive corner of the rink.
- Select two defensemen and a forward line to start. They set up as if there is a face-off in one of the offensive zone circles.
- While the players are standing in their face-off positions, softly shoot a puck past the near-boards defenseman into the neutral zone.
- The players react by retreating to the neutral zone area.
- The near-boards defenseman retrieves the puck and quickly makes a cross-ice pass to his partner, who is in a more defensive position in the middle of the ice and gliding backwards.
- The near-boards winger and center turn through the middle of the neutral zone following the movement of the cross-ice pass.
- The far side winger skates quickly to the far boards and stands stationary, ready for a transition pass from the defense.
- The players regroup when the far defenseman passes the puck to the stationary far winger who in turn feeds the puck to either the center or the near winger.
- The play is complete when the forward line makes an offensive play on the net.

Key Teaching Points
- Encourage the opposite defenseman to be in a more defensive position than his partner to ensure the cross-ice pass is not intercepted.
- Emphasize to the forwards that they should circle towards the cross-ice pass with sticks ready to receive a forwarding pass.

EXPANSION

The far defenseman makes a pass to any of the forwards in the neutral zone.

Both defensemen follow the regroup play inside the offensive zone. Pass a puck to one of them and have them pass it back and forth with control, standing stationary inside the blue line. On a whistle, one defenseman takes a low shot while all three forwards are jammed in front of the crease blocking the goalie's view and looking for a tip-in or rebound.

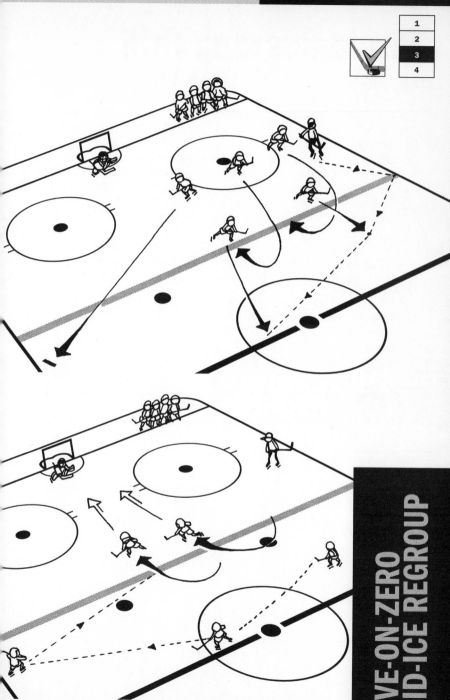

FIVE-ON-ZERO MID-ICE REGROUP

Circle Regroup Drill

Objective

To develop proper swing movement with the puck, developing short passing opportunities

Description

- Line up four defensemen on the corner face-off dots.
- Position other players on diagonal blue lines with pucks.
- The first player at the blue line passes the puck to the close defenseman and then swings back into the defensive zone.
- The defenseman passes to his partner, and the partner passes back to the first player.
- Begin both ends at the same time; once the skater has received the return pass he skates down the ice for a one-on-zero play on the goalie.

Key Teaching Points

- Encourage players to circle deep into the defensive zone for easy pass receiving.
- Emphasize the importance of the timing of the swing.
- Emphasize a deep swing into the defensive zone by the skater to allow for an easier return pass.

EXPANSION

Play a two-on-zero swing—one player from each side, starting from one end of the ice at a time.

CIRCLE REGROUP DRILL

Two-on-One Transition Drill

Objective
To develop high-speed transitions from regrouping to offense

Description
- Position defensemen on the four corner face-off dots, and the other players line up on the boards at both blue lines.
- The first player in both lines at one end coordinates a pass to one of the stationary defensemen, then circles deep into the defensive zone for a return pass.
- On receiving the return pass, the two players skate to the other end with the defenseman following up to the centerline.
- Once over the far blue line, the puckhandler passes to the opposite end defenseman and both forwards swing again.
- The forwards again receive a return pass and complete the drill by playing a two-on-one against the first defenseman.
- Once the offensive players have crossed the centerline, the next group begins.

Key Teaching Points
- Encourage high tempo and good passes.
- Promote deep swings into the defensive zone for easy pass receiving.

EXPANSION
Two defensemen follow the play up the ice for a two-on-two situation.

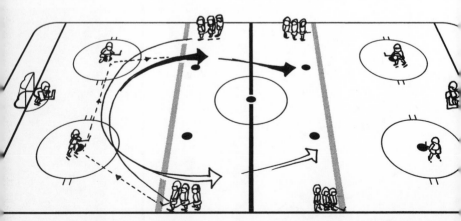

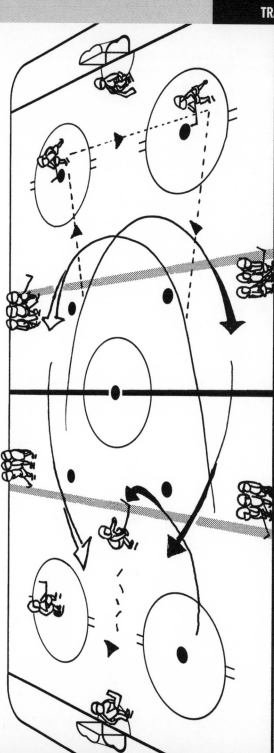

**TWO-ON-ONE
TRANSITION DRILL**

Five-on-Zero Regroup Drill

Objective
To encourage strong mid-zone puck control of the puck

Description
- Line up five players in center face-off positions.
- Begin play with one of the five-on-zero breakout options from the Five-on-Zero Breakout Drill on pages 72–73 of Book 3, *Team Drills*.
- Forwards skate hard down the ice passing the puck past the far blue line.
- The defensemen skate hard to the centerline, then turn backwards and skate back to the top of the defensive zone circles.
- The forwards swing through the offensive zone and curl back, passing the puck back to one defenseman, who quickly makes a defense-to-defense pass.
- The forwards retreat back down the ice, swing again in the defensive zone, receive a return pass from the defenseman and finally swing again, attacking offensively down the ice for a three-on-zero offensive play on the far net.
- Once the third transition has taken place, pass one of the defensemen an additional puck. He skates to inside the blue line, passing the puck and then stops, taking a shot on goal once the offensive play has been completed for a tip-in or a rebound.

Key Teaching Points
- This is a good progression from the Five-on-Zero Breakout Drill, pages 72–73 in Book 3, *Team Drills*.
- Encourage the defense to always follow up the play quickly.
- Encourage the forwards to come back deep to enable effective passes.

1
2
3
4

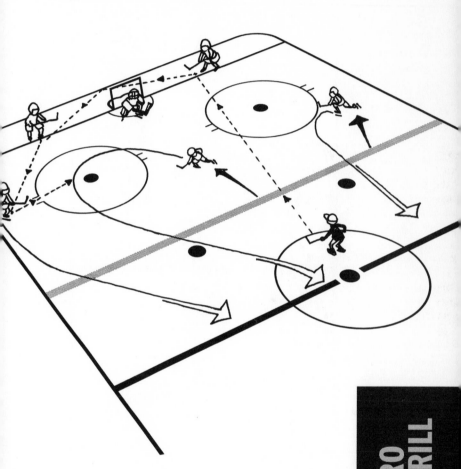

**FIVE-ON-ZERO
REGROUP DRILL**

continued...

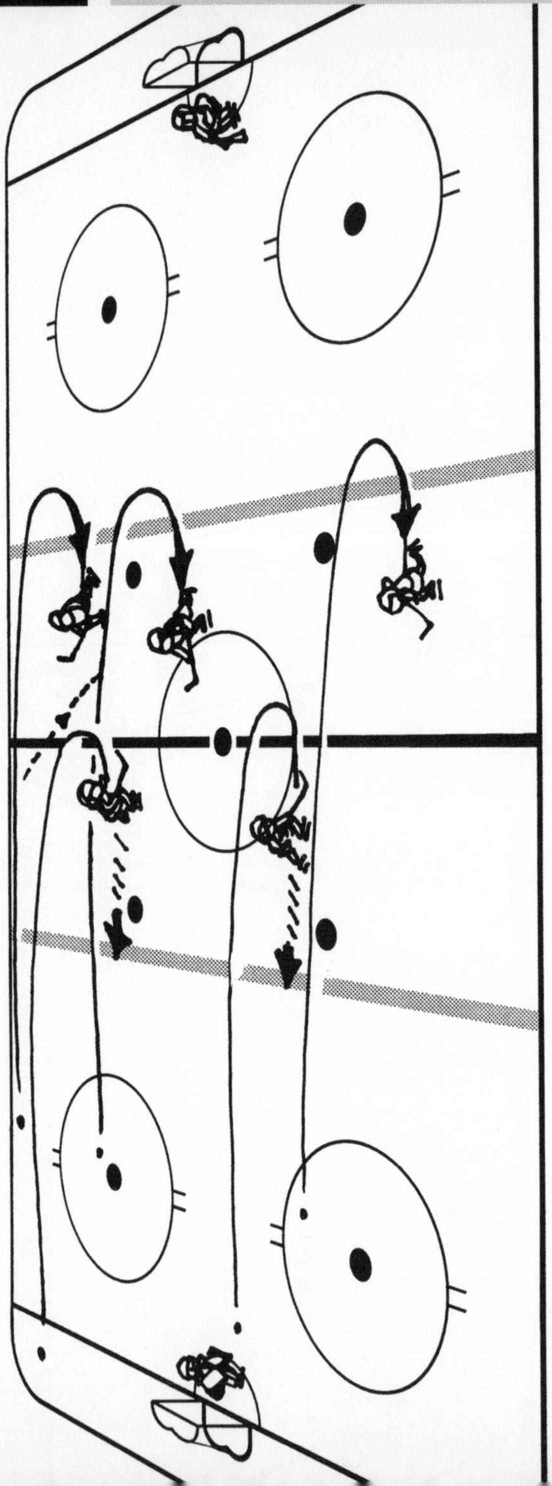

**FIVE-ON-ZERO
REGROUP DRILL**

Three-on-Two Three Times

Objective
To encourage good puck movement with transition skating

Description
- Pair up defensemen at the corner face-off dots and at the centerline. Group forwards into lines and stand on the boards in the mid-ice zone.
- The first forward line starts by passing a puck to the corner face-off defenseman.
- The defenseman quickly makes a cross-ice pass to his partner. The forwards swing into the defensive zone, receive the puck and skate down the ice for a three-on-two against the opposing defensemen who have joined the play at the centerline.
- Once past the blue line, the forward who has control of the puck passes to one of the opposing defensemen.
- Again there is a defense-to-defense pass; the forwards swing in the offensive zone, receive the return pass, then skate down the ice for a second three-on-two play.
- Repeat the transition once again, and finish the drill with a final three-on-two play on the far net.
- The final defensive pair rests, and a new defensive pair and line begins.

Key Teaching Points
- Encourage play at high speed.
- Encourage forwards to swing in the same direction as the puck movement.
- Encourage defensemen to follow up the play and join the offensive attack.

1
2
3
4

EXPANSION

Forwards stay in front of the offensive net after their
three-on-two play, maintaining good crease position and
having one of their defensemen take another shot on
goal for a tip-in or a rebound.

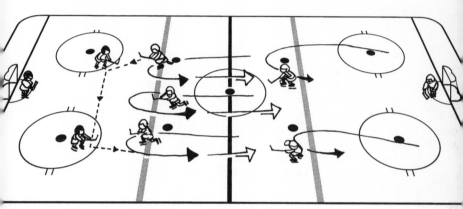

THREE-ON-TWO
THREE TIMES

Four-on-Four Quick Change Scrimmage

Objective
To encourage high-speed skating and puck movement with quick player transition from rest to active playing mode

Description
- Divide players into two teams, and position each team in a players' bench.
- Four players from each team begin a scrimmage—two defensemen and two forwards.
- Begin play by dropping the puck or shooting it into a corner.
- Blow the whistle after 30 to 45 seconds; players must immediately skate quickly off the ice.
- Four new players enter the ice surface and immediately begin play against a new opposition where the live puck is located. There are no face-offs throughout the drill.
- Play continues at a high tempo, with open-ice passing and high-speed skating.
- If one team scores, shoot the puck behind the net and resume play.

Key Teaching Points
- Encourage high-speed skating with quick reaction to the whistle signalling player changes.
- Encourage players to always skate hard all the way to the bench at the end of a shift in order to promote more effective player changes.

EXPANSION

#1. Only three players per team play during the scrimmage.

#2. Use a rule that new players cannot enter the ice until an existing player reaches the player's bench and is fully off the ice. This option reinforces the importance of players skating full speed all the way to the bench during a "change on the fly."

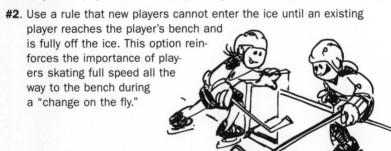

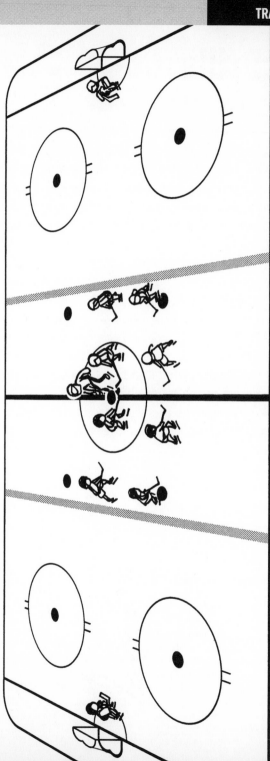

FOUR-ON-FOUR QUICK CHANGE SCRIMMAGE

Goalie Drills

Definition—*the techniques and skills necessary to become a reliable, proficient goaltender*

AS THE GAME OF HOCKEY BECOMES MORE COMPETITIVE at older age levels, the outcomes of games are often determined by small differences in the talent or preparation of the two teams involved. Nowhere is that more important than in the goaltending position, the last bastion of defense before a goal is scored.

Although most hockey coaches have experience in playing minor hockey, only a small proportion has played goal and has a good idea of how to properly train a netminder. In many situations in minor hockey, goalies are often neglected during practice simply because none of the coaches feels qualified to organize a goalie-only drill. Often the scope of goalie-specific drills simply includes a coach taking warmup shots prior to the start of the team shooting drills.

Goaltenders, like all hockey players, improve their skills remarkably when challenged with well-organized and skill-specific drills during practice. Many experienced goaltending coaches believe that the most important skill a coach can teach a young goaltender is that of developing a proper stance, with feet and body square to the puck, knees bent and stick on the ice. Repetition of this

stance in shooting and goalie-specific drills is a great way to reinforce good habits in the minds of goaltenders, both young and old. From a team standpoint, the most experienced coaches realize the importance of goalie-related drills during practice and incorporate them into every session that they plan.

The following selection of drills includes those that two goalies can perform on their own, those that can be done with a coach and those where the whole team can participate.

When developing team and individual hockey skills, goalie skills are often overlooked. This is primarily because few coaches have experience in playing the position. Even an experienced head coach who has some valuable input for the goaltenders often does not have much time to spend one-on-one with these important players. Coordinating drills for the entire team takes precedence. In fact, most minor hockey teams do not even assign a volunteer to be a goalie coach and, as a result, these young players are often left to fend for themselves.

As in the offensive and defensive positions in hockey, there are several fundamental skills that every goaltender must develop. These skills include:

1. Skating
2. Agility
3. Puckhandling
4. Passing
5. Positional Awareness
6. Up and Down Skills
7. Crease Movement
8. Glove Skills
9. Rebound Control

GOALIE DRILLS

NINE KEY GOALIE SKILLS

The first four skills are the same as for any player, even though these skills are often used in ways unique to goaltenders. The goalie should therefore work on many of the same drills as the rest of the team, since these team drills are similarly designed to improve a goaltender's overall skill. Later in each practice, goalie-specific drills can be included to develop the remaining five skills.

Skating

Young players who have not yet learned to skate well are often asked to play goal, since their lack of skill in skating may not be so obvious in goal and will not be detrimental to the team. Spectators are likely to notice a speedy winger darting for an open puck to score the winning goal long before they notice how fluidly a goalie plays the angles or how deftly a goalie controls a puck dumped into the defensive corner. Both of these goalie-specific skills require good skating skills.

The ability to skate well allows goaltenders to cover the corners of the crease more effectively and to become like a third defenseman on dump-ins. They can get to the loose puck and quickly begin the team transition back to offense. One of the most important skills for a goalie is the ability to come out of the crease in order to cut down the angles for oncoming shooters. Strong skaters move more quickly and also keep their pads in better defending position while striding back into the crease in anticipation of a shot or deke.

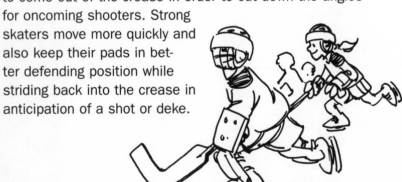

As players progress into higher levels of hockey, goaltenders have to be some of the strongest skaters on the team simply because of the significantly increased equipment weight! Strong legs and catlike agility allow goalies to move easily throughout the crease area despite their burden of bulky, heavy pads.

Agility

No other hockey player is required to go from a standing to prone position with as quick and full recovery as a goaltender must. Skate saves, butterfly maneuvers, stacking the pads, poke check dives—all of these skills require great agility, especially when considering the weight and bulk of goalie equipment. A goalie may have fantastic glove reaction and solid positional play; however, in a dynamic, fast-moving game like hockey where offensive chances often come in multiples, the ability to recover from one play and regain full control for the next is vital. For the netminder, no skill is more important than agility.

Agility is defined as the ability to change directions quickly while maintaining control. The very nature of goaltending demands a high degree of agility, whether recovering to a standing position after a butterfly save or sprawling across the crease to stop a rebound. With the rising cost of ice time, it is advisable to begin showing young goalies simple, inexpensive and enjoyable drills both on and off the ice that, when done regularly, can improve their agility. An intuitive coach will organize dryland sessions for goaltenders to improve agility, balance and coordination so that regular ice time can be directed to puck-related skills.

Puckhandling

It is often assumed that a goalie's responsibility is to stop the puck. Once that is done, then the defensemen or forwards take over and clear the puck to a teammate or out of the zone. That is often the case with many teams where the goalie has not developed strong puckhandling skills. However, a goaltender who has good puck-handling skills gives the team an added offensive advantage, especially when beginning transitions from defense to offense by controlling the puck adeptly.

Passing

The highlight reels of National Hockey League goaltenders in the 1950s and '60s are always interesting to watch. All great athletes, these goalies played their position almost as if there was a rope tied between their legs and the net. Rarely would they venture far from the confines of their net to handle a puck. Their job was a relatively simple one: just stop the puck when it was shot. With the evolution of a high-speed game involving counterattacks and transition plays in the defensive and neutral zone as pivotal components of the game, the role of a goalie has expanded. A team whose goalie can handle the puck well and start an offensive play with crisp, accurate passes to teammates has a valuable advantage over its opposition. No longer are goalies solely assigned the role of puck stopper; they have become valuable sixth members of the offensive forces.

Unlike defensemen and forwards who usually rely on weight transfer to make hard and accurate passes, a goalie's strategy for passing is slightly different. The angle between a player's stick blade and the shaft of the stick is called the "lie." Skating players usually use a lie 5 or 6 stick compared with an almost upright lie 13 goaltender stick. Because goalies have such an upright stick to help stop the puck, it is more difficult for them to sweep the blade of the stick across the ice using proper weight transfer when making a pass. You will notice that goalies will more frequently use a snap pass, using only arm strength to make a quick and accurate pass to a teammate. Very little body weight transfer occurs with a snap pass. This is one of the main reasons why young goalies have a difficult time passing the puck; they have not developed sufficient upper body strength. There are some instances in higher levels of hockey where a goalie will attempt a long-distance pass or an end-to-end shot on an open net and will use a weight transfer technique, but this is the exception rather than the rule. Weight transfer when passing the puck is a valuable skill for players in all hockey positions, including goal.

Positional Awareness

Being aware of one's proper position on the ice is a valuable skill for all players, but for goaltenders, this skill is essential. If a forward is caught out of position, a three-on-two play may result. For a defenseman, poor positional awareness may give up a scoring opportunity in the slot area. In the case of goalies, being in the wrong position results in an easy tap-in goal or open net shot that can negatively change the momentum of a game.

It is common to see goalies who shine in practice but have greater difficulty during a fast-paced game.

For years they have practiced the same moves, techniques and strategies that have made them fundamentally strong goalies. Unfortunately, almost all of this experience comes from controlled practice settings, where they are used to having time to properly set up for each shot. Awareness of their location in the net is easy when goalies have ample time to establish where they are in the crease relative to the goal posts.

Great goaltenders often challenge themselves to react in practice to being out of position in order to be better prepared when this inevitably happens in a game. It is interesting to watch one of the best goalies in the National Hockey League, Dominic Hasek. Nobody could ever accuse Dominic of having a methodical, traditional approach to stopping the puck. It is an uncanny awareness of his position in the crease relative to the shooter that allows him to often pull off incredible saves. The situations where he has time to set up and be totally prepared for an oncoming shot become even easier since he is constantly working on his positive awareness.

Up and Down Skills

In the more elite levels, goalies must have the ability to make all the routine saves and the majority of the difficult saves. What sets apart the truly great goaltenders from all the rest is the ability to make the game-saving play, which causes a shift in the momentum of a game and thus frustrates the opposition. These plays are successful because the goalie has the ability to recover quickly from a sprawling play or a scramble in front of the crease and return to a standing, ready position.

Up and down skills are especially difficult for young goaltenders because they require good leg strength, which many young players have not yet developed adequately. Therefore, it is important to focus on improving technique while waiting for young muscles to grow in size and strength.

There are two main ways for goalies to get back up to a set position after being down on their knees. Goalies can perform a two-legged hop by pushing down on the front of their skates while forcefully straightening their knees, thus effectively hopping back up to their feet. This is the best technique because it is done at a high speed, and goalies stay in better balance during the maneuver.

Young goalies may not have the leg strength to try this. They often opt for a one-legged method where they first raise one foot properly to be flat on the ice, follow that with an upward body movement, and finally bring the last foot under them in order to rise into a standing position. This is a much slower technique but one that may be used by young goalies or by those who are tired at the end of a high tempo game.

Crease Movement

The first time hockey players compete on international-sized ice surface, they realize that the game is much different than on most North American rinks. The forwards love the extra ice in the corners and behind the net because they are havens for nifty puckhandlers and are usually out of the reach of their defensive opposition. On the other hand, the wider lanes down the side of the boards challenge defensemen. They must adjust their angles for one-on-one plays and odd-man situations. However, it is the goaltenders who have to modify their normal shot setup the most. They have to be aware of cutting down potentially even greater angles and being even more aware of the increased puck movement and play behind the net.

With the significant increase in the offensive zone size, goalies must be even more skilled at moving laterally as well as forward and back to counter this apparent offensive advantage. Since the National Hockey League has increased the amount of ice behind each goal line, movement in the crease continues to become an even more important goaltending skill.

Glove Skills

One of hockey's most exciting moments is when a goaltender makes a dazzling glove save, robbing the opposing forward of what was apparently a sure goal. Both blocker and catching gloves are valuable components of a great goalie's defensive arsenal. Although glove speed and quick reflexes are important in developing an intimidating upper body advantage, anticipation and good angling skills are vital for goalies to increase their chances to make great glove saves.

Rebound Control

The vast majority of great goalies rarely get beat on the first shot on goal during a rush. They have the time to set up their angles properly and, unless the opposing player makes a fabulous shot, the advantage certainly is on the goaltender's side. However, once the first save is made, any advantage is negated if the puck is rebounded to the dangerous slot area just in front of the crease. In this situation, opposing forwards have the goalie potentially off balance and unable to prepare easily for a second shot. Although this is where a skilled defenseman can help the goalie by clearing loose rebounds out of the slot, goalies who are able to minimize dangerous rebounds by directing the puck into the corners are doing themselves a valuable service! As is the case with preventing injuries, preventing a potential scoring opportunity is a great deal more effective than having to react to one. When defensemen and goalies communicate, they can ensure that it is virtually impossible for the opposition to get an "easy goal."

A Final Word about Goalie Skills

In many levels of amateur hockey, goalies are often overlooked when it comes to involving them in practice. Most often this is because the coaching staff do not feel comfortable teaching goalie skills or may not have adequate assistance on the ice during practice. Assigning an assistant coach the responsibility of working with the goaltenders is an effective solution to making sure these important players get the attention they both need and deserve.

There are many skills that young goaltenders need to master in order to reach their full potential. The drills in this section are a comprehensive selection of drills that will make coaching goalies an easy and successful experience.

Side Shuffle Technique

Objective

To develop lateral movement technique while staying square to the puck and maintaining proper angles

Description

- Goalie begins with the outside skate inside one of the goalposts.
- With small sliding movements, the goalie slowly works his way across the crease as if he is pushing snow with the blade of his skate.
- Goalie keeps both skates square to the puck facing directly outward during these movements.
- Goalie maintains a ready position for stopping shots with gloves always in the proper position and stick on the ice.

Key Teaching Points

- Encourage goalies to keep their weight over their skates at all times, with feet and body staying square to the puck.
- Promote small, progressive skating movements across the crease while still maintaining a ready position.
- Encourage goalies to maintain a "quiet" upper body that does not move up and down while shuffling.

SIDE SHUFFLE
TECHNIQUE

T-Push Technique

Objective
To develop quick lateral movement technique across the complete width of the net

Description
- Goalie begins the drill with the outside skate inside one of the goal-posts.
- Goalie angles the inside skate 90°, pointing towards the other post, and making a "T" with his skates.
- With the back knee bent, the goalie makes a leg push to glide across the full width of the net.
- Goalie must keep his upper body still, with no bobbing up and down while pushing.
- Goalie repeats the maneuver back across the goalmouth, with good balance throughout.

Key Teaching Points
- Encourage goalies to keep their weight over their skates at all times.
- Promote proper angling of the lead skate prior to push off.
- Encourage the goalie to keep both skates on the ice, opening and closing the body as quickly as possible.

| 1 |
| 2 |
| 3 |
| 4 |

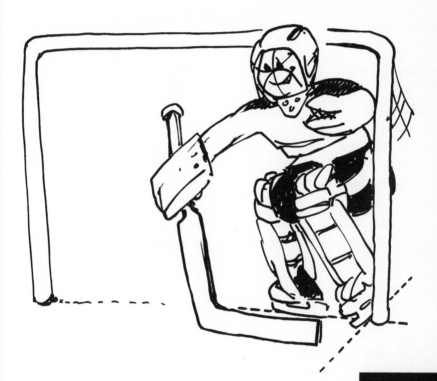

T-PUSH
TECHNIQUE

Telescoping Out and Back Technique

Objective
To develop good forward and backward movement while staying prepared for a shot

Description
- Goalie begins the drill deep in the crease in ready position.
- He uses C-cut leg movements out of the crease area towards the coach who is in the mid-slot area.
- Goalie then stops and retreats back deep into the crease.
- Goalie remains ready for a shot throughout the skating distance by keeping his eyes and chest up while moving.

Key Teaching Points
- Encourage goalies to keep knees bent, moving with minimal weight transfer by extending their legs using a C-cut movement.
- Promote the proper angling technique depending on puck position.
- All movement requires minimal skating strides and minimal weight transfer.

TELESCOPING OUT
AND BACK TECHNIQUE

Down & Up Technique

Objective

To develop agility with quick return to the feet after being on the ice

Description

- Stand in front of the net with the goalie in the ready stance in the crease.
- Tap a stick on the ice as a signal for the standing goalie to go down quickly to his knees onto the ice.
- The goalie tries to return to a standing position as quickly as possible, keeping his chest up.
- Have the goalie perform the drill for three, five, or ten repetitions before changing goalies.
- Allow ample rest between sets.

Key Teaching Points

- Encourage quick balance recovery.
- Ensure that the goalie is prepared for a shot as he returns to his feet.
- Encourage goalie to keep his stick on the ice whenever possible.

EXPANSION

Goalie performs the drill without a stick to increase the challenge of regaining good position and balance after being on his knees on the ice.

Skating Skate-Save Technique

Objective

To develop proper technique for a lateral skate save

Description

- Goalie begins in a ready stance position in the crease.
- Tap a stick on the ice as a signal, pointing to the right or left corner.
- The goalie reacts by angling his skate outward and extending his leg to the side indicated.
- Quickly repeat the signal, varying left and right, for five to ten repetitions.
- Goalies switch after two or three sets of repetitions.
- Allow ample rest to ensure full intensity.

Key Teaching Points

- Encourage good initial positioning with weight always over skates.
- Encourage quick skate movements.

EXPANSION

Goalie plays without a stick to encourage better balance.

1
2
3
4

Half-Split Save Technique

Objective
To develop the proper technique for a split save

Description
- Goalie begins in a ready stance in the crease.
- Tap a stick on the ice as a signal, pointing to the right or left corner.
- Goalie reacts by bending one knee, extending the other leg outward in a rotated manner.
- Goalie must recover quickly and resume a ready stance in the crease.
- Repeat the drill, varying left and right, for five to ten repetitions.
- Goalies switch after two or three sets of repetitions.
- Allow ample rest to ensure full intensity.

Key Teaching Points
- Encourage good balance when going down on the ice.
- Encourage good leg extension on the kick leg.

1
2
3
4

COACH

TAP
TAP

HALF-SPLIT SAVE
TECHNIQUE

Half-Butterfly Save Technique

Objective
To develop the proper technique for a half-butterfly save

Description
- Goalie starts in a ready stance in the crease.
- Tap a stick on the ice as a signal, pointing to the right or left corner.
- Goalie reacts by going down on both knees and rotating one leg out in a butterfly position.
- Goalie must recover quickly and resume a ready stance in the crease.
- Repeat the drill, varying left and right, for five to ten repetitions.
- Goalies switch after two or three sets of repetitions.
- Allow ample rest to ensure full intensity.

Key Teaching Points
- Encourage good balance when going down on knees.
- Promote proper hip rotation to develop a half-butterfly.
- Ensure the goalie keeps his stick on the ice in a ready position.

**HALF-BUTTERFLY
SAVE TECHNIQUE**

Butterfly Save Technique

Objective
To develop the proper technique for a butterfly save

Description
- Goalie starts in a ready stance in the crease.
- Tap a stick on the ice as a signal, pointing to the right or left corner.
- Goalie reacts by going down on both knees and rotating both legs out in a butterfly position.
- Goalie should go forward onto his knees rather than simply dropping to his knees.
- Goalie must recover quickly and resume a ready stance in the crease.
- Repeat the drill for five to ten repetitions.
- Goalies switch after two or three sets of repetitions.
- Allow ample rest to ensure full intensity.

Key Teaching Points
- Encourage good balance when going down, landing on both knees at the same time.
- Promote proper hip rotation to develop the butterfly position.
- Encourage goalie to present a big upper body to the shooter, with the torso erect.

1
2
3
4

**BUTTERFLY
SAVE TECHNIQUE**

Double Leg Stack Technique

Objective
To develop the proper technique for a double leg stack

Description
- Goalie starts in a ready stance in the crease.
- Tap a stick on ice, pointing to the right or left corner.
- Goalie reacts by going down on his side, while stacking his pads towards the corner indicated.
- Goalie must recover quickly and resume a ready stance in the crease.
- Repeat the drill, varying left and right, for five to ten repetitions.
- Goalies switch after two or three sets of repetitions.
- Allow ample rest to ensure full intensity.

Key Teaching Points
- Encourage good balance when going down into a pad-stacked position.
- Encourage good extension of the bottom arm to maximize ice coverage on a shot.
- Encourage the goalie to snap his bottom leg out under his top leg to maintain a symmetrical position.

DOUBLE LEG STACK TECHNIQUE

Letter Drill

Objective
To develop good crease movement

Description
- Goalie starts in a ready stance in the crease.
- Select a letter in the alphabet and have the goalie trace it in the crease area while moving quickly. The example shown here is the letter "W," where the goalie practices proper goalpost coverage.
- Once the goalie has traced the letter three times, choose another letter and repeat the drill before switching goalies. Suitable letters to use are "V," inverted "V," inverted "Y," "L," reverse "L," "N," inverted "T," "Z" or reverse "Z."
- Allow ample rest to ensure full intensity.

Key Teaching Points
- Encourage goalie to keep his weight over his skates at all times, with feet and body staying square to the puck.
- Promote small, progressive skating movements around the crease area while still maintaining a ready goalie position.
- Encourage goalie to maintain a "quiet" upper body that does not move up and down while he is moving.

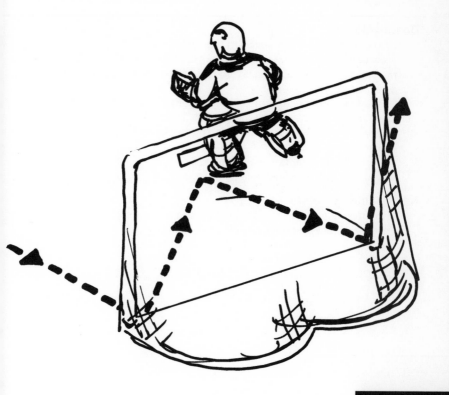

LETTER DRILL

Skipping Drill

Objective

To develop the proper balance, coordination, and leg strength

Description

- Goalie starts in a ready stance in the crease.
- A coach or goalie partner, who is down on one knee at the top of the crease, slowly slides his stick through the crease like a windshield wiper.
- Goalie reacts to the stick movement by jumping up and over the stick every time it comes through the crease.
- Goalie must recover quickly from each jump and resume a ready stance in the crease.
- Continue the drill for five to ten jumps, slowly increasing the number as the season progresses and as the goalie's endurance improves.

Key Teaching Points

- Encourage good ready position with eyes and chest up.
- Encourage bent knees on take-off and landing.

SKIPPING DRILL

Angle Drill

Objective
To develop good lateral movement and goalpost awareness

Description
- Skate back and forth in front of the net as if you are stickhandling with a puck.
- Goalie follows your movement, always maintaining the proper angle.
- Watch that the goalie protects the goalpost on a sharp angle shot.

Key Teaching Points
- Encourage small lateral shuffle steps both ways.
- Encourage the goalie to always keep his stick in front of his skates.
- Encourage the goalie to move directly to the goalpost on each side.

EXPANSION

Stickhandle a puck while skating, and try shots on the goalie from various angles in front of the net.

1
2
3
4

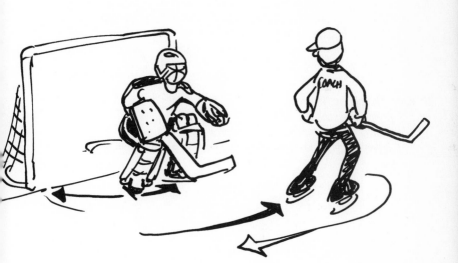

ANGLE DRILL

Down & Up Drill

Objective
To develop good positional recovery for a save after being down on the ice

Description
- Goalie starts in a ready stance in the crease.
- Tap a stick on the ice to signal the goalie to quickly go down onto both knees.
- Goalie immediately and quickly returns to a ready position.
- Once he resumes a ready position, take a shot on goal.
- Start with five times up and down, then increase to seven, nine, eleven or more as the goalie's stamina increases.
- Allow sufficient rest between sets to ensure proper recovery technique.

Key Teaching Points
- Encourage foot quickness.
- Promote good balance and recovery.
- Speed, agility and balance are the keys to a successful save recovery.

1
2
3
4

DOWN
& UP DRILL

T Drill

Objective
To improve agility in the crease

Description
- On a whistle, the goalie slides from a goalpost to the center of the crease.
- He then skates out to the front edge of crease and back deep into the net.
- From there he slides over to the other goalpost and back to middle net position.
- Once the goalie is back in a ready position in the middle net position, take a shot on goal.
- Allow sufficient rest between sets to ensure proper technique.

Key Teaching Points
- Encourage good lateral and forward movement.
- Ensure that this is a full-speed drill.
- Encourgage speed and tight pad control.

T DRILL

Pad-Stacking Drill

Objective

To develop proper pad-stacking technique

Description

- Goalie starts in a ready position in the middle of the net.
- Point with a stick to a corner of the net.
- Goalie stacks his pads in the direction that the stick is pointing.
- Goalie must recover quickly to a standing ready position, first by getting up on one knee with his stick on the ice and gloves up in ready position.
- Once the goalie is back in a ready position, take a shot on goal.
- Repeat, varying sides, four to six times quickly.
- Allow sufficient rest between sets to ensure proper technique.

Key Teaching Points

- Encourage good pad position.
- Emphasize the importance of good balance.
- Encourage the goalie to snap his bottom leg out under his top leg to maintain a symmetrical position.

PAD-STACKING DRILL

Tight Circle Pass and Shot

Objective
To develop good puck awareness and quick lateral movement

Description
- Goalie positions himself in the net while four or five players form a semi-circle directly in front of the net, 3 to 5 meters (9 to 15 feet) out.
- Players have one puck that they pass quickly among each other.
- Occasionally a player takes a shot on goal, and all players prepare for a possible rebound.
- Goalie must follow the rapid puck movement, while staying ready for a shot.
- After two or three shots the players rotate, moving to new shooting positions.
- Allow sufficient rest for the goalie to ensure high-quality reactions to the puck movement.

Key Teaching Points
- Encourage good body position square to the player with the puck.
- Encourage quick lateral movement while maintaining proper pad and glove position.

TIGHT CIRCLE
PASS AND SHOT

Behind-the-Net Control Drill

Objective

To develop proper positioning techniques when the puck is controlled behind the net

Description

- Goalie starts in a ready stance in the middle of the net.
- Position two lines of players in one corner; one line with pucks.
- The first player with a puck skates behind the net while the first player from the other line skates in front of the net.
- The puck carrier fakes back and forth behind the net a few times, then attempts a pass to his teammate in front.
- Goalie follows the puck carrier's movement and adjusts his position accordingly. He should try to block the pass if possible with proper stick positioning outside the post area.
- The player takes a shot on goal if the pass gets through, and he looks for a rebound.
- The next pair begins once the goalie resumes a ready position.

Key Teaching Points

- Encourage good use of peripheral vision, always looking over the shoulder that is closest to the post.
- Ensure goalie's skate is always tight to the near post.
- Encourage proper use of the stick for poke checking and pass interception.

Mirror Drill

Objective
To reinforce proper body, pad and glove movement techniques

Description
- Two goalies face each other at one end of the rink.
- One goalie leads the drill; the other follows as quickly as possible, trying to mirror the leader's movements.
- The movements should include pad stacking, butterfly, up & down, standing skate save, half-split save, half-butterfly, high glove save, high blocker save.
- After 20 seconds, the goalies switch roles.
- Allow sufficient rest between sets to ensure a high-speed drill and good quality of movement.

Key Teaching Points
- Encourage goalies to stay in a ready position at all times.
- Encourage good balance and recovery.

1
2
3
4

MIRROR DRILL

Turkey Shoot

Objective
To practice angle shots and to improve endurance

Description
- Goalie starts in the net with five shooters arranged at various positions in the offensive zone.
- Give each shooter five pucks and a number from one to five.
- Call a number to signal the appropriate shooter to take a wrist shot.
- The goalie makes the save and recovers for the next shot.
- Control the drill by calling out numbers so that the goalie gets proper recovery time.
- After each player has taken all five shots, switch goalies.
- Allow ample rest time to ensure high practice intensity.

Key Teaching Points
- Encourage the goalie to maintain good positioning.
- Encourage quick reaction time.

TURKEY SHOOT

Puck-Clearing Drill

Objective
To build strength in passing and clearing the puck out of the zone

Description
- Goalie starts in a ready stance in the middle of the net.
- Position two lines of shooters, one on each side of the near blue line.
- Set up a pylon just inside the blue line in the middle of the ice.
- One player shoots the puck into the end zone around the boards.
- The goalie controls the puck and passes it to the far side player, who has skated deep into the defensive zone to the hash mark and has positioned himself with his back directly towards the boards.
- The near side player circles into the middle for a second pass, skates around a mid-ice pylon and returns to the same goalie for a shot on goal and possible rebound.

Key Teaching Points
- Ensure correct forehand and backhand technique.
- Ensure stable stickhandling.
- Encourage the goalie to keep his head up.
- Emphasize quick control and strong and accurate passing by the goalie.

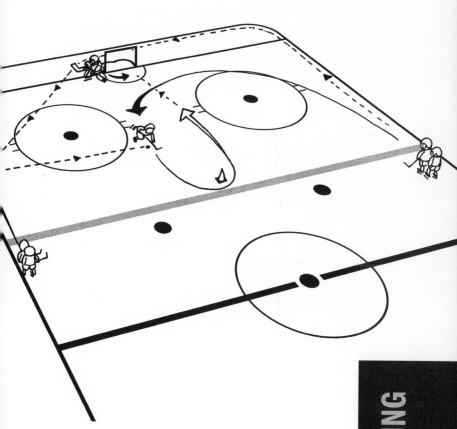

PUCK-CLEARING DRILL

Behind-the-Net Attack

Objective
To develop good puck awareness and quick lateral movement

Description
- Players line up in one corner of the ice.
- The first player starts the drill by skating from the corner to behind the net with a puck.
- Goalie tracks the skater's position and keeps his near skate directly on the post.
- Skater moves back and forth behind the net and then attacks the front of the crease.
- Goalie must follow the puck movement, while staying prepared for an offensive attack.
- Skater options from behind the net include a quick puck jam, far side high shot, spin to the front and shot, and five hole shot while skating across the crease.

Key Teaching Points
- Encourage the goalie to set up properly with his skate tight to the near post.
- Encourage quick lateral movement while maintaining proper pad position.

EXPANSION

Goalie plays without a stick, thus encouraging even better anticipation and skate movement.

1
2
3
4

BEHIND-THE-NET ATTACK

Quick-Turn-Around Saves

Objective
To develop improved crease awareness

Description
- Position a player or coach 5 meters (15 feet) in front of the net with several pucks.
- Goalie positions himself in the middle of the crease, facing directly into the net.
- On a signal, either a verbal cue or a stick tapped onto the ice, the goalie quickly turns to face the shooter who takes a shot as the goalie tries to regain his crease positioning and bent leg ready position.
- The drill is quickly repeated five times in succession after which the goalies switch to allow for ample rest.
- Be sure to vary the shots from side to side and from top to low corners.

Key Teaching Points
- Encourage the goalie to rotate quickly with knees bent.

EXPANSION

Goalie assumes a specific position after each rotation, namely, using the standing skate save, half-split save, half-butterfly save, butterfly save, or the double-pad stack save.

TAP
TAP

Three-Shot Pad Stack

Objective
To improve pad stacking technique and proper recovery

Description
- Position two players or coaches with pucks 5 meters (15 feet) out from the front of the net diagonally to ensure angled shots.
- Goalie lines up towards one of the shooters, and the drill starts with a direct shot on goal.
- After making the save, the goalie quickly slides across the goal crease stacking his pads in an attempt to stop a shot coming from the second shooter.
- As soon as that save is made, the goalie must recover to his feet and immediately slide back across the crease stacking his pads in an attempt to stop the final third shot from the first shooter.
- Allow the goalie ample rest before starting again. Repeat the drill five successive times before switching goalies.

Key Teaching Points
- Encourage the shooters to keep the shots low.
- Encourage the goalie to quickly recover from the pad-stack position to a full standing and ready position.

EXPANSION

Goalie uses other save variations such as the butterfly save or half-split save to stop the second or third shots.

Butterfly Save

1
2
3
4

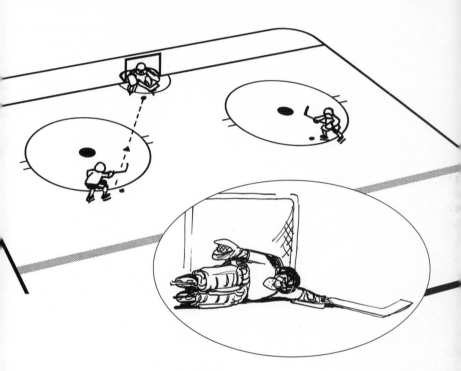

Half-Split Save

**THREE-SHOT
PAD STACK**

Five-Shot Variation Drill

Objective

To challenge goalies with a variety of shots

Description

- Set up five stations at each end of the rink as shown.
- Begin the drill with a wrist shot from Player #1.
- Player #2 curls from the corner and shoots from a tight angle immediately after the goalie stops the first shot.
- Player #3 then skates around the back of the net and attempts to jam his puck into the net on the far side.
- Player #4 follows, taking a wrist shot from the left blue line area.
- Finally, Player #5 attempts a one-on-zero breakaway on the goalie to complete the drill.

Key Teaching Points

- Encourage the shooters to use wrist shots and hit the net.
- Encourage the goalies to react quickly across the crease in preparation for each shot.
- It is important that the timing of the shots gives the goalie little chance to regain proper position in his crease. The objective of the drill is to improve his ability to quickly react to a variety of challenging shots.

EXPANSION

Two sets of shooters perform the drill before allowing the goalie to have a rest.

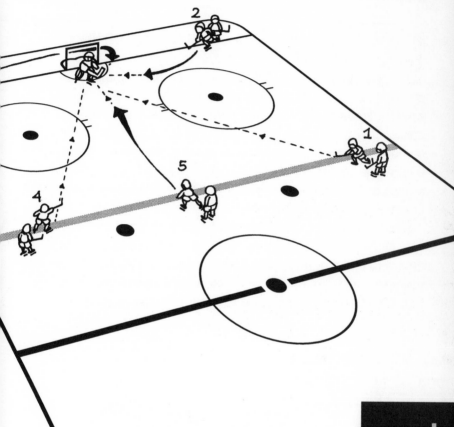

FIVE-SHOT VARIATION DRILL

Games

Definition—*on-ice activities that develop individual player skills while having fun*

IF THERE IS ONE THING THAT A COACH CAN DO FOR HIS players that will be more important than any other aspect of his teaching, it is to make sure that the players enjoy the game. As a player progresses through higher levels of the game, increasing pressure to perform causes many young hockey players to retire from hockey far too early in their lives. A coach can never guarantee that players will turn out to be the best in the world, but he can guarantee that they will gain a passion for the game. The way to do that is by making every practice and game fun for all!

There are many games that can be done at practice that not only challenge players to develop their skills, but also create an environment of enjoyment and success in sport. The games that follow offer just a few. You may know many more, or you may wish to adapt these games to your own coaching style.

Whatever you do, however, always try to end the practice on a positive note. These fun games can help you to do just that. After all, which would you rather your players remember during the time between practices—a gut-wrenching conditioning skate or an enjoyable challenging game that they work at with full intensity. Both drills provide a conditioning element for your players, but while one will be tolerated, the other will be eagerly anticipated!

GAMES

Prisoner's Base

Objective
To develop skating and agility skills

Description
- Move one net to the corner of the rink, 3 meters (9 feet) from the boards.
- Lay all sticks in an opposing corner out of the way as they are not required in this game.
- The area between the net and the boards is the prison and it is guarded by one of the coaches who is the prison guard.
- The other coaches take the role of police officers. They skate hard to touch all the players once the whistle goes to start the game.
- If a police officer or prison guard touches a player, then that player skates directly to prison.
- The player must stay in jail until another player sneaks in and touches him, releasing him from prison.
- Allow prison breaks occasionally to keep the flow of the game going.

Key Teaching Points
- Challenge players to make quick turns and accelerations.
- Encourage the strategy of helping other skaters.
- Have fun, fun, fun.

EXPANSION

More experienced players become prison guards and police officers.

PRISONER'S BASE

British Bulldog

Objective

To develop agility and speed

Description

- Line up all the players on a goal line.
- Coaches line up in the mid-ice zone between the blue lines as opposition.
- Coaches yell, "British Bulldog," and the players try to skate quickly to the opposite end of the rink.
- Coaches try to touch the players as they skate through the mid-ice zone.
- When a player is touched, he joins the middle-zone opposition.
- The last skater untouched is the winner.

Key Teaching Points

- Alternate and use fun names, such as Cats and Mice, Men in Black or Shredder Shredder.
- Challenge players to test their skating limits.
- Have fun, fun, fun.

EXPANSION

Play the game with pucks. Each player begins the drill with a puck and stickhandles down the ice quickly. Coaches try to steal a puck from a player and must put it into a net to turn the skater into the middle-zone opposition.

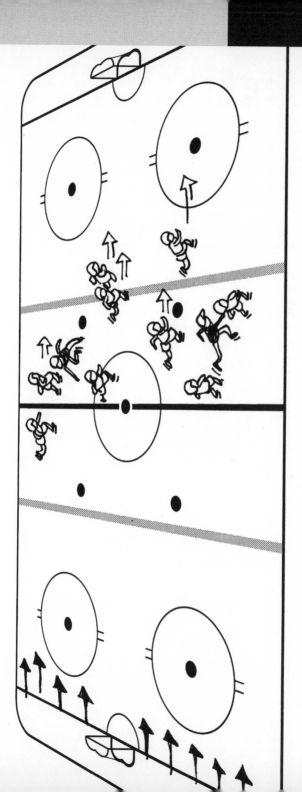

BRITISH
BULLDOG

Chain Tag

Objective
To develop teamwork and strategy

Description
- Choose two players or coaches to be the first chain. They must hold hands and skate quickly around the ice attempting to touch a free player.
- If a player is touched, then he must join the chain by holding hands.
- Once there are four players in a chain, they split into two chains of two players each.
- The game continues until all players are part of a chain.
- The last player to join a chain is the winner.

Key Teaching Points
- Emphasize cooperation and teamwork.
- Have fun, fun, fun.

CHAIN TAG

Frozen Tag

Objective
To develop agility and teamwork

Description
- Choose coaches or three or four players to be "it."
- On a whistle, all players skate away from those who are "it."
- If they are tagged, then players must freeze with arms outstretched.
- Other players can rescue a "frozen" player by skating under his arm, allowing him to resume play.
- Challenge players to make tight turns, quick sprints and accelerations.

Key Teaching Points
- Encourage quick skating and good peripheral awareness.
- Have fun, fun, fun.

FROZEN TAG

Train Race

Objective
To develop team cooperation and balance

Description
- Divide players into four groups.
- Position four pylons spread out across the top of the offensive circles.
- Line up the groups behind the defensive-zone hash marks in line with each of the pylons.
- The front player acts as a conductor and cannot skate; his hands must stay on his knees. The rest of the group are the engines and must skate quickly.
- On a whistle, all trains skate down the ice, around a pylon, and return to the starting line.
- The first team back to the defensive-zone hash mark wins.
- If a train falls apart, then the players must stop and repair it in order to resume skating.

Key Teaching Points
- Encourage controlled skating.
- Promote working together as a unit.
- Have fun, fun, fun.

EXPANSION

Only the last player skates. Rotate players after each cycle so all players have the opportunity to be the last skater before the drill concludes.

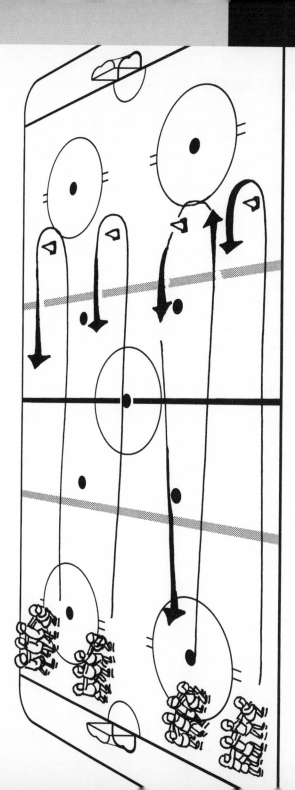

TRAIN RACE

Three-on-Three Half-Ice Mini Hockey

Objective
To develop tactical defensive and offensive playmaking skills

Description
- Divide players into teams of three; two teams begin play at each end of the ice.
- Begin with a face-off and play three-on-three competition inside each blue line.
- The team that gets puck possession must take the puck outside the blue line to begin their offensive plays.
- When a turnover occurs, the team must again take the puck outside the blue line in order to start an offensive play.
- Players try to skate to openings on the ice, practicing playmaking skills.
- Set a time limit of five to ten minutes per game. The winning team then plays against a team who challenges them.
- Players who are not involved in the three-on-three games in the end zones can practice agility skating, face-off drills and long passing in the neutral zone.

Key Teaching Points
- Encourage good defensive positioning in front of the net.
- Encourage quick transitions from defense to offense.
- Encourage players to move to openings on the ice.

THREE-ON-THREE HALF-ICE MINI HOCKEY

Showdown

Objective
To develop shooting and faking skills

Description
- Gather all players at center ice with pucks.
- Skating at full speed, each player takes one penalty shot on each goalie.
- If a player scores no goals or only one, then that player goes to one side of the rink.
- If a player scores two goals, then that player goes to other side of the rink.
- Have a sudden-death showdown if some players are tied with two goals.
- Disqualify a goal if the player skates at less than full speed towards the net.

Key Teaching Points
- Players must perform penalty shots at full speed.
- The shooter should attempt to wait for the goalie to make the first move.

SHOWDOWN

Half-Ice Baseball

Objective

To develop quick and accurate passing skills

Description

- Divide players into four teams, with two teams playing in both ends of the rink.
- The team that is up to bat lines up in one corner of the rink.
- The other team is in the infield and is spread out inside the blue line.
- The first hitter shoots the puck somewhere inside the blue line. If the puck goes outside the blue line, then it is a foul ball and must be hit again.
- The infielders must retrieve the puck, pass it three times, and then try to score.
- Once he makes a hit, the hitter skates quickly around a pylon located outside the blue line and returns across the goal line.
- If the infielders score before the hitter crosses the goal line, then that is an out and the next hitter is up to bat.
- If the hitter crosses the goal line before a goal is scored, then that is a home run.
- After three out, the teams switch positions.
- Keep score to encourage fun and competitive spirit.

Key Teaching Points

- The hitter must skate at full speed.
- Encourage the infielders to work together to pass and attack the net.

Mid-Ice Three-Puck Challenge

Objective
To develop quick offensive power and regrouping strategy

Description
- Position the nets in the center of both blue lines, facing each other.
- Choose two teams and begin near the boards at the two blue lines across the ice from each other.
- The first three skaters in each line form a team; they have three pucks placed on the blue line beside them.
- On a whistle, each team of three takes one puck and skates to the opposite net and tries to score.
- If the goalie makes a save, then he quickly clears the puck from the net.
- Once a team scores a goal, they quickly skate back to the original blue line and get the next puck.
- The team makes a second offensive play, and when they have scored twice, they quickly skate back to the original blue line and retrieve the final puck.
- The team makes a third offensive play, and when they have scored three times, all three players skate quickly back over the original blue line.
- The first team with all their players over the blue line is the winner.
- The next two groups of three skaters begin once the pucks are set up again.

Key Teaching Points
- Encourage rapid and effective offensive thrust.
- Encourage the development of a team strategy to advance the puck on net.

EXPANSION

Reverse the goal nets so that they face away from each other, making it much harder to score and defend against.

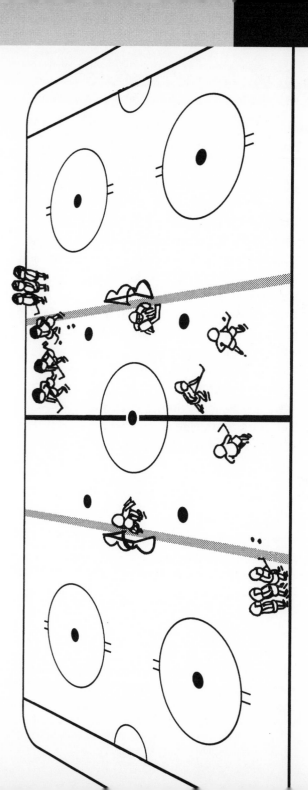

MID-ICE THREE-
PUCK CHALLENGE

Appendix

Practice Plans

This appendix contains four different practice plans, each one aimed at developing a particular skill. These can be cut out or photocopied and used as a quick practice plan or can be adapted to your own personal style. Each practice plan is outlined for a 60-minute practice and includes suggested time frames for each drill. Each includes a warmup, a skating drill and then several drills to develop a particular skill. Practice sessions conclude with a time for closing remarks and a short cooldown skate.

It is important to finish every practice with a couple of positive words about the good things that were done on the ice. It is a great way to have the players leave the ice in a positive frame of mind. Conversely, if the effort at practice was poor, closing off the session with a word about the things that the players could do better at the next practice still leaves them with a positive reference and good direction for a more productive session in the future.

The cooldown laps are a good way of showing young players that, from a physiological standpoint, slowly cooling off with stretches and half-speed striding is a good way of allowing their muscles to recover after a hard workout.

A blank practice plan is included here. It is reproducible and can be used to develop your own personal practice plans.

Hockey Practice Plan _____

OBJECTIVE: _____

Drill Name	From	To	Key Points
1.			
2.			
G—			
3.			
G—			
4.			
G—			
5.			
G—			
6.			
7.			
8.			
9.			

– Hockey Practice Plan 1 –
OBJECTIVE: Team Play

Drill Name	From	To	Key Points
1. Double-Circle Warmup[1]	0	5	stretch/agility/warmup
2. Five-Circle Skating[1]	5	10	crossover skating technique
3. Shadow Drill[1] –Side Shuffle Technique[4]	10	15	agility/skating/stickhandling
4. Defensive Zone Positioning[3] –Skipping Drill[4]	15	25	defensive zone awareness
5. Attack the Triangle[2] –Quick-Turn-Around Saves[4]	25	35	close quarters stickhandling
6. 3-on-2 Three Times[4]	35	45	transition skating
7. 3-on-3 Mid-Ice 3-Puck Scrimmage[4]	45	55	offense/defense transition
8. Stick-Steal Race[1]	55	58	agility/skating
9. Closing/Two Cooldown Laps	58	60	feedback/cooldown

minutes

Notes:

[1] Book 1: *Skating Drills for Hockey*
[2] Book 2: *Puck Control Drills for Hockey*
[3] Book 3: *Team Drills for Hockey*
[4] Book 4: *Advanced Drills & Goalie Drills for Hockey*

– Hockey Practice Plan 2 –
OBJECTIVE: Power Play/Penalty Killing

Drill Name	From	To	Key Points
1. Double-Circle Warmup[1]	0	5	stretch/agility/warmup
2. Skating Fundamentals[1]	5	10	skating technique
3. 1-on-1 Stationary Keepaway[3] –Half-Butterfly Save Technique[4]	10	15	checking/power
4. Power Play Offensive Breakouts[4]	15	30	full-ice man-advantage breakouts
5. 5-on-4 Offensive Power Play[4]	30	40	offensive zone passing
6. 4-Man Box Rotation[4]	30	40	consistent box formation
7. 4-on-4 Quick Change Scrimmage[4]	40	50	high-tempo play, quick change
8. Caboose Race[1]	50	58	power development
9. Closing/Two Cooldown Laps	58	60	feedback/cooldown

minutes

Notes:

[1] Book 1: *Skating Drills for Hockey*
[2] Book 2: *Puck Control Drills for Hockey*
[3] Book 3: *Team Drills for Hockey*
[4] Book 4: *Advanced Drills & Goalie Drills for Hockey*

– Hockey Practice Plan 3 –
OBJECTIVE: Advance Passing

| | minutes | | |
Drill Name	From	To	Key Points
1. Double-Circle Warmup[1]	0	5	stretch/agility/warmup
2. Eight-Dot Skating[1]	5	10	agility
3. Shadow Drill[1] –Butterfly Save Technique[4]	10	15	crossovers, skating
4. Blue Line Horseshoe Drill[2]	15	25	passing
5. 4-Corner Box Passing & Shot[2]	25	30	passing/shooting
6. Full-Ice Horseshoe Drill (with Options)[2]	30	40	stickhandling
7. Diagonal Pass & Shoot[2]	40	50	passing & receiving
8. Half-Ice Baseball[4]	50	58	agility/fun
9. Closing/Two Cooldown Laps	58	60	feedback/cooldown

Notes:

[1] Book 1: *Skating Drills for Hockey*
[2] Book 2: *Puck Control Drills for Hockey*
[3] Book 3: *Team Drills for Hockey*
[4] Book 4: *Advanced Drills & Goalie Drills for Hockey*

– Hockey Practice Plan 4 –
OBJECTIVE: Skating and Checking

Drill Name	From	To	Key Points
1. Double-Circle Warmup[1]	0	5	stretch/agility/warmup
2. Full-Lap Stick Relay[1]	5	10	speed/coordination
3. Stick-Jump Drill[1]	10	15	agility/fun
4. Bucket Relay[1]	15	22	skating speed
5. Defense-to-Wing-to-Center Pass & Shoot[2]	22	30	positioning/team play
6. 5-on-0 Breakout Drill[3]	30	40	team play
7. Around-the-Net Angle Drill[3]	40	45	checking technique
8. Direct Pinning Drill[3]	45	50	checking technique
9. Full-Ice 1-on-1 Drill[3]	50	55	checking
10. Prisoner's Base[4]	55	58	agility/fun
11. Closing/Two Cooldown Laps	58	60	feedback/cooldown

minutes

Notes:

---

[1] Book 1: *Skating Drills for Hockey*
[2] Book 2: *Puck Control Drills for Hockey*
[3] Book 3: *Team Drills for Hockey*
[4] Book 4: *Advanced Drills & Goalie Drills for Hockey*

Drill Index

Acknowlegments

A special thanks goes to the members of the Titans from Sherwood Park, Alberta, their friends, friends of Randy Gregg and parent volunteer Elliot Chiles for helping with the photo shoot for the covers of these books.

Top Row (L to R): Matthew Willard, Randy Gregg, Jared Phillips, Trevor Brophy
Middle Row (L to R): Jared Semen, Jade Chiles, Michael Budjak
Bottom Row (L to R): Jeremy Rockley, Cassidy Monaghan, Donald Anderson, Brandon Chunick, Chase Elliott, Alec Chomik
Goalie: Travis Bambush

We couldn't have done it without you!